DISCOVER
Skills for Life

Merita L. Thompson, Ed.D.
Professor, Department of Health Education
Eastern Kentucky University
Richmond, Kentucky

Johanna F. Strange, Ed.S.
Assistant Professor
Model Laboratory School
Eastern Kentucky University
Richmond, Kentucky

American Guidance Service, Inc.
Circle Pines, Minnesota 55014-1796

CONTRIBUTING AUTHORS

Dr. Ruth Ann Althaus
Professor, Health Education
Illinois Benedictine College
Lisle, Illinois

Dr. David J. Anspaugh
Professor, Health Science
Memphis State University
Memphis, Tennessee

Barbara H. Waldner, MSW
Licensed Clinical Social Worker
Certified Chemical Dependency
  Counselor
Acra, Boldt, Durham, Waldner &
  Weir, Assoc.
Lexington, Kentucky

REVIEWERS

The publisher wishes to thank the
following reviewers of *DISCOVER:
Skills for Life* for their helpful com-
ments. Their assistance has been
invaluable.

Reading:
Louise P. Matteoni
Regent
The University of the State of New
  York Regents College
Formerly President, New York State
  Reading Association
Bayside, New York

Health and Science:
Dr. Michael Amantea
National Institutes of Health
Department of Pharmacology
Bethesda, Maryland

Bonnie Benard
Drug Education Research Analyst
Prevention Resource Center
Springfield, Illinois

Patricia Eckert
Substance Abuse Prevention
  Consultant
Carbondale, Illinois

Dr. Joe D. Exline
Director of Science
Virginia Department of Education
Richmond, Virginia

Mike Jackson
Middle School Science
Camp Lejeune Dependents' School
Camp Lejeune, North Carolina

Dr. Len Tritsch
Specialist, Health Promotion
Salem, Oregon

Curriculum and Instruction:
Dr. Charles Coble
Dean, School of Education
East Carolina University
Greenville, North Carolina

Dr. Karen Lind
Department of Early and Middle
  Childhood Education
University of Louisville
Louisville, Kentucky

Gregory Marshall
Elementary Appraisal Specialist
Clear Creek Independent District
League City, Texas

Donna Oliver
Center for Science Education
Clarion University
Clarion, Pennsylvania

Claribel Rockhill
Barclay School
Brockport Central Schools
Brockport, New York

Additional:
Sylvia Abdul-Haqq
Consultant
Student Substance Abuse Program
  for Drug Free Schools
Philadelphia, Pennsylvania

Sharon Alexander
Dade County Public Schools
Miami, Florida

Mary D. Bonilla
Vena Avenue School
Los Angeles, California

Diane DeNinno-Brodkey
Hazeltine Avenue School
Los Angeles, California

Valerie Garcia
Monterey Elementary School
Colorado Springs, Colorado

Mary Ann George
Education Consultant
Rivertown Consultants
Lansing, Michigan

Terry Goldberg
Mission Trail Elementary School
Leawood, Kansas

Cynthia Knowles
Western New York Regional Drug
  Education Coordinator
Board of Cooperative Educational
  Services
Mount Morris, New York

David J. Mathews
Counselor/Coordinator, Adolescent
  Services
Amherst H. Wilder Foundation
St. Paul, Minnesota

Harriette Meriwether
Drug Free Schools Coordinator
Pittsburgh Public Schools
Pittsburgh, Pennsylvania

Gerri Moore
Director, Health and Physical
  Education
Houston Independent School
  District
Houston, Texas

Michaelene Pepera
Center for Peace and Conflict
  Studies
Wayne State University
Detroit, Michigan

Teri Telepak
Educational Consultant, Prevention
  Specialist
Greensburg, Pennsylvania

Marti White
Drug Free School Coordinator
Orange County School District
Orlando, Florida

ACKNOWLEDGMENTS
Illustrations
Pages iv, 9, 10, 16, 30, 40, 43, 44,
  46, 47, 48, 49, 50, 51 by Darcy A.
  Tom

ISBN 0-7854-0323-X   Product Number 15701
A 0 9 8 7 6 5 4 3 2 1

Table of Contents

Unit 1   **Building Self-Esteem** 1

Lesson 1   What Makes You Special? 2
Lesson 2   What Makes You Worthy?..................................6
Lesson 3   What Are Your Feelings? 8
Lesson 4   How Can You Show Your Feelings? 10
Lesson 5   Who Can Help When You Have Feelings? 12
Lesson 6   How Can You Show Warm Feelings? 14

Unit 2   **Becoming Informed About Drugs** 16

Lesson 7   What Helps When You Are Sick? 18
Lesson 8   When Do You Need Medicine?.......................22
Lesson 9   How Do You Use Medicines Safely? 24
Lesson 10   What Drugs Are Not Medicines?....................26
Lesson 11   What Is Drug Dependency? 28

Unit 3   **Building Decision-Making
                 and Relationship Skills** 30

Lesson 12   How Can You Make Healthy Decisions? 32
Lesson 13   Why Are Your Decisions Important to Others? 36
Lesson 14   How Can You Treat Others Well? 40
Lesson 15   How Can You Be Responsible? 42

Unit 4   **Building Violence Prevention Skills** 44

Lesson 16   What Is Violence? 46
Lesson 17   How Can You Handle Strong Feelings? 48
Lesson 18   What Are Ways You Can Get Along? 50

UNIT 1

The world is full of people.

But every person is special.

What Makes You Special?

No one else is just like you.

You are very **special.**

You can help.

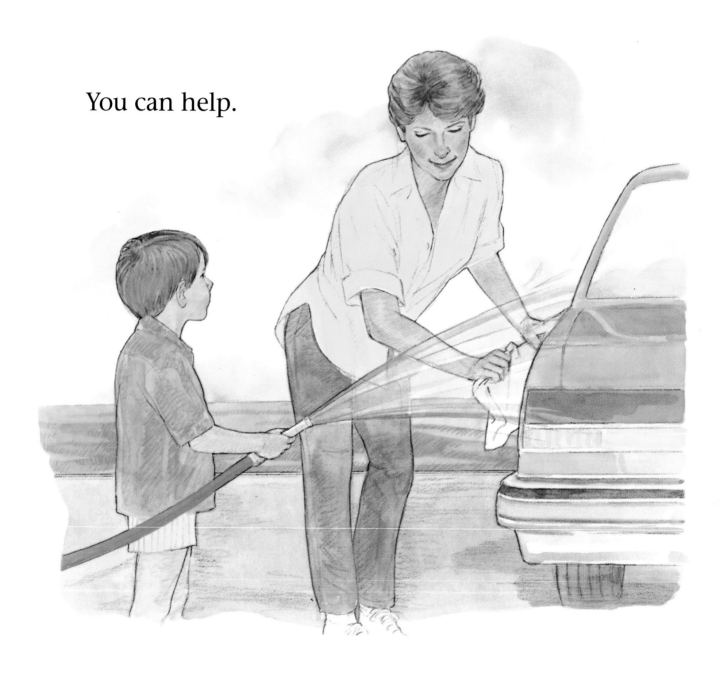

You are loved. You can love.

What Makes You Worthy?

You are a person. All people deserve love.

You are **worthy** because you are you!

What Are Your Feelings?

You have many feelings.

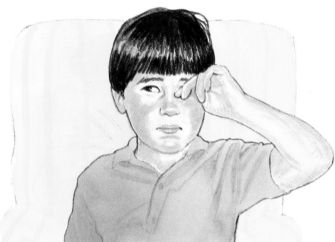

sad

happy

angry

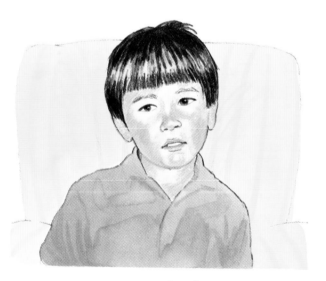

worried

You may feel happy or sad. Your feelings are OK.

How Can You Show Your Feelings?

It is all right to cry.

It is all right to sigh.

It is all right to laugh
and shout.

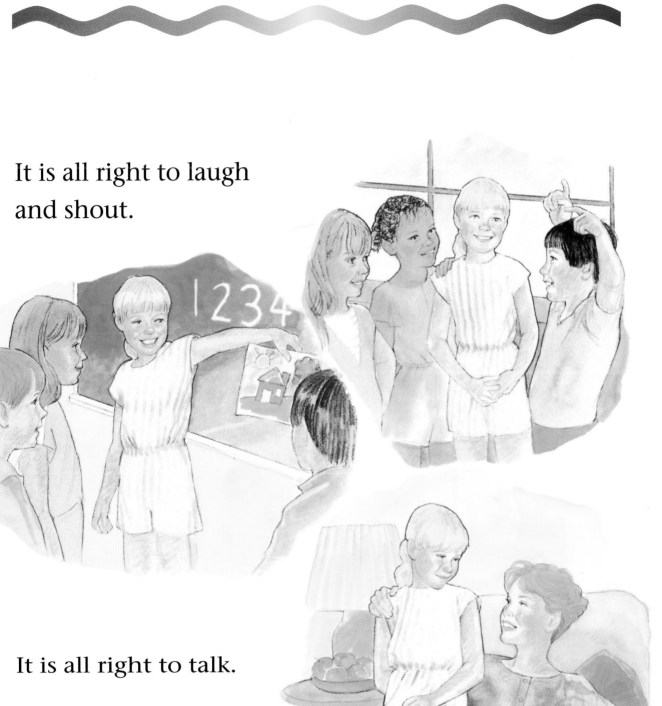

It is all right to talk.

It is all right to hug.

Who Can Help When You Have Feelings?

Friends can share sad or happy feelings with you.

Family members can share feelings, too.

How Can You Show Warm Feelings?

A hug can say, "You are special."

A smile can say, "I like you."

You can say, "I love you."

UNIT 2

Taking care of your body is important.

You can say no to drugs that might hurt you.

What Helps When You Are Sick?

Everyone gets sick sometimes.

You may need rest.

You may need **medicine.**

Medicines are **drugs** that can help the body to work better.

Never decide by yourself that you need medicine.

When Do You Need Medicine?

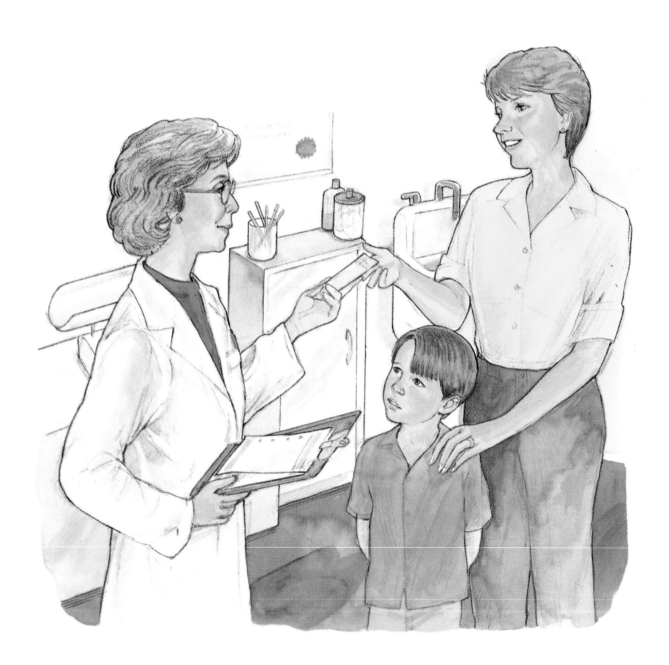

Who decides that you need medicine?
Sometimes doctors give you medicine.

Only a caring adult should decide.

How Do You Use Medicines Safely?

You should never take medicine by yourself.
Medicine should be kept in a safe place.

You should never take someone else's medicine.

What Drugs Are Not Medicines?

Some drugs are **poison.**

They can make you very, very sick.

These things have drugs in them.
They can be harmful to children.

What Is Drug Dependency?

Some people who often use drugs become **drug dependent.** They feel a strong need for the drugs.

Drug dependent people are sick.
But they can get help.

UNIT 3

Every day you make decisions.

Your decisions are important.

12
LESSON

How Can You Make Healthy Decisions?

You can make **decisions**.

Healthy decisions help to keep you safe and well.

Think carefully before you decide.

Others who care about you can help you to decide.

Why Are Your Decisions Important to Others?

You are important to your family.

You are important to your friends.

Healthy decisions can help
you to get along with others.

Healthy decisions can help
you to take care of yourself.

14
LESSON

How Can You Treat Others Well?

You can decide to be nice to
others. They can be nice to you.

You can decide to get along with others.
You can work together.

How Can You Be Responsible?

You can decide to be **responsible.**

You can follow rules.

You can **respect** others.

UNIT 4

You can decide to get along with others.

People feel good when they get along.

What Is Violence?

Violence is doing things to hurt people.

Hitting others is one kind of violence.

Harming another person's things is violence.

46

Words can hurt, too.

Saying mean things to others can cause violence.

Violence hurts everyone.

How Can You Handle Strong Feelings?

All people feel angry sometimes.

Violence is not a healthy way to show anger.

Talking with someone can help.

Solving problems can help, too.

Violence can cause worry and sad feelings.

You can ask for help.

You can talk with someone who cares.

What Are Ways You Can Get Along?

Getting along makes people happy.

You can share.

You can be kind to others.

50

You can say you are sorry.

You can talk about a problem.

You can follow rules that keep people safe.